Albert Einstein

A Buddy Book
by
Rebecca Gómez

Publishing Company

VISIT US AT

www.abdopub.com

Published by Buddy Books, an imprint of ABDO Publishing Company, 4940 Viking Drive, Suite 622, Edina, Minnesota 55435. Copyright © 2003 by Abdo Consulting Group, Inc. International copyrights reserved in all countries. No part of this book may be reproduced in any form without written permission from the publisher.

Printed in the United States.

Edited by: Christy DeVillier
Contributing Editors: Matt Ray, Michael P. Goecke
Image Research: Deborah Coldiron
Graphic Design: Jane Halbert
Cover Photograph: Library of Congress
Interior Photographs/Illustrations: Denise Esner, Getty Images, Library of Congress, PhotoEssentials

Library of Congress Cataloging-in-Publication Data

Gómez, Rebecca.
    Albert Einstein / Rebecca Gómez.
       p. cm. — (First biographies. Set III)
    Includes index.
    Summary: An introduction to the life and work of the twentieth-century physicist whose theory of relativity revolutionized scientific thinking.
    ISBN 1-57765-946-5
     1. Einstein, Albert, 1879-1955—Juvenile literature. 2. Physicists—Biography—Juvenile literature. [1. Einstein, Albert, 1879-1955. 2. Physicists. 3. Scientists.] I. Title.

QC16.E5 G675 2003
530'.092—dc21
[B]

                                                              2002074675

Table Of Contents

Who Is Albert Einstein?

Albert Einstein was a great scientist. He studied energy, matter, and natural forces of the world. This kind of science is called physics.

Einstein discovered many new things. His discoveries gave people a better understanding of the world. This is why people call Albert Einstein a genius.

Albert Einstein

Growing Up

   Albert Einstein was born on March 14, 1879, in Ulm, Germany. His parents were Hermann and Pauline. His little sister was Maja. Albert's family moved to Munich, Germany, when Albert was a baby.

Albert with his sister Maja.

Young Albert loved to read books and learn. He learned about math from his Uncle Jacob.

But young Albert did not like school. His teachers did not allow students to ask questions. They wanted students to remember facts. Young Albert wanted to understand these facts.

One day, Albert's father gave him a gift. It was a compass. Young Albert wondered what made the compass always point north. Albert enjoyed trying to understand new things.

A compass is a tool that helps people find their way.

Leaving Germany

In 1894, Albert Einstein's family moved to Italy. Albert went to school in Switzerland. He enjoyed studying physics. At school, Albert met Mileva Maric.

In 1903, Albert married Mileva. He worked at the Swiss Patent Office in Bern, Switzerland. He enjoyed studying physics when he was not working.

Albert Einstein studied physics.

A Young Scientist

Albert Einstein came up with new ideas about light, matter, time, and energy. He wrote five papers about his ideas in 1905.

A German science journal printed Albert's papers. Other scientists read about Albert's ideas. Schools invited him to give talks. The University of Geneva honored Albert for his important ideas.

The Einstein Tower in Potsdam, Germany, was built in honor of Albert Einstein.

In 1909, Albert and Mileva moved to Zurich, Switzerland. He began teaching physics at the University of Zurich. They moved again two years later. In 1911, Albert began teaching at the German University in Prague, Austria-Hungary.

Switzerland was Einstein's home for many years.

Einstein's Famous Theory

In 1914, Albert Einstein began teaching in Berlin, Germany. World War I began that year. Albert's wife and two sons moved back to Switzerland. Later, Albert and Mileva's marriage broke up.

Albert kept studying physics. He discovered new things about gravity. Einstein discovered ways that gravity changes time, light, and space. These ideas are part of Einstein's theory of relativity. This theory is one of the biggest discoveries in science.

$$E = mc^2$$

E=mc2 is a famous part of Einstein's special relativity theory.

Albert worked too hard and became very sick in 1917. Elsa Lowenthal took care of him. In 1919, she and Albert married.

Albert Einstein with his wife Elsa Lowenthal

Later in 1919, an English scientist did a special experiment. This experiment showed that Albert's theory of relativity was true. Many people did not understand Albert's theory. But he became famous anyway.

Einstein's Fame

Schools across the world invited Albert Einstein to speak. In April 1921, Albert and Elsa went to America. Reporters greeted Albert as soon as he arrived. Americans were excited to meet Albert Einstein.

Albert and Elsa traveled to many countries.

Albert and Elsa visited New York, Boston, Chicago, and other cities. Einstein helped to raise money to open a university.

In 1922, Albert and Elsa went to Japan. Sailing home, they discovered that Albert won the Nobel Prize for physics.

Albert Einstein (third from left) with other Nobel Prize winners in 1933.

Moving To America

In 1933, a new set of leaders ruled Germany. These leaders were the Nazis. The Nazis persecuted Jewish people like Albert Einstein. Germany was not a safe place for Jewish people anymore. That year, Albert and Elsa moved to the United States.

Adolf Hitler (front) was the leader of the Nazis.

Albert and Elsa moved to Princeton, New Jersey. Albert worked at the Institute for Advanced Study. He and Elsa enjoyed the United States. President Franklin D. Roosevelt invited them to the White House.

In 1935, Elsa became sick. She died in 1936.

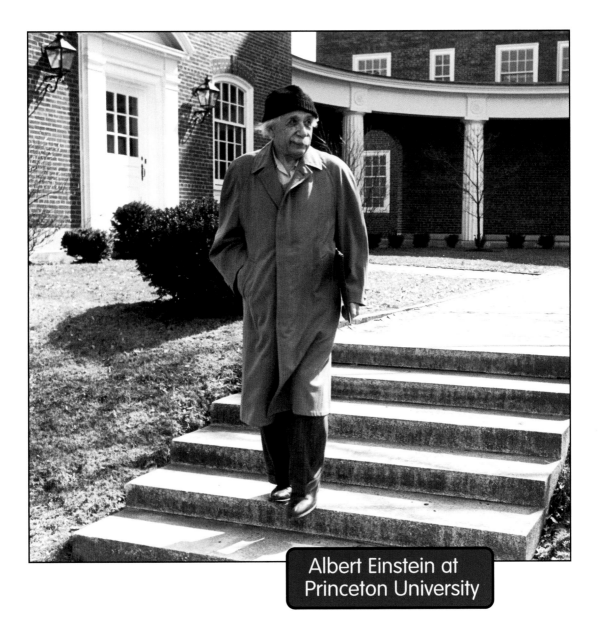

Albert Einstein at Princeton University

A Genius

Albert Einstein stopped working for the Institute for Advanced Study in 1945. But he kept studying physics. Albert also began speaking out against war. He believed the world could live peacefully as one country.

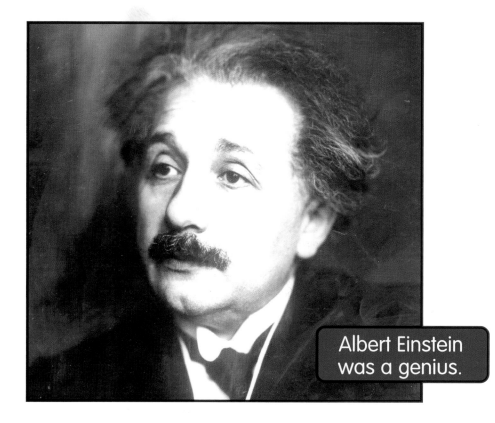

Albert Einstein was a genius.

On April 18, 1955, Albert Einstein died. The world has not forgotten this great scientist. Today, Albert Einstein's picture is on posters, in magazines, and in movies. People remember him as a great genius.

Important Dates

March 14, 1879 Albert Einstein is born.

1894 The Einstein family moves to Italy.

1900 Albert graduates from the Swiss National Polytechnic.

1903 Albert marries Mileva Maric.

1905 Albert writes five important papers about his discoveries in physics.

1919 Albert marries Elsa Lowenthal.

1922 Albert discovers he has won the 1921 Nobel Prize in physics.

1933 Albert and his wife move to the United States.

1936 Albert's wife, Elsa, dies.

1940 Albert becomes an American.

April 18, 1955 Albert Einstein dies in Princeton, New Jersey.

January 2000 *Time* magazine names Albert Einstein "Person of the Century."

Important Words

energy power that allows a natural force to do work. Heat is one form of energy.

experiment a special test. People often learn something from an experiment.

genius a person that is uncommonly creative and smart.

gravity a natural force that pulls objects to the ground.

persecute to make people suffer.

physics the study of energy, matter, and natural forces.

theory a law of science.

Web Sites

Einstein—Image and Impact
www.aip.org/history/einstein
See pictures of Albert Einstein and learn more about his life.

Einstein
www-groups.dcs.st-and.ac.uk/~history/Mathematicians/Einstein.html
Find more information about Albert Einstein here.

Index